Round the World
WORKING

The Save the Children Fund
and Macmillan Education

This is a map of the world.
There are five continents – Europe,
Asia, America, Africa and
Australasia.

On this map you can see some of the
countries in the world which come
into this book.

Key

1 AUSTRALIA
2 BANGLADESH
3 CANADA
4 CHINA
5 ICELAND
6 INDIA
7 INDONESIA
8 IRAN

9	ISRAEL	17	RUSSIA
10	JAPAN	18	SRI LANKA
11	KENYA	19	SWEDEN
12	MALAYSIA	20	TANZANIA
13	NIGERIA	21	THAILAND
14	NORWAY	22	UNITED KINGDOM
15	PAKISTAN	23	RIVER AMAZON
16	SAUDI ARABIA	24	LAKE CHAD

Going to work

In the past, the man in the family went out to work. Sometimes the children did too. In Victorian England children were sent down coal mines, and helped sweep chimneys.

Sometimes the wife also went out to work. But she usually stayed at home and worked in the house.

In some countries women had a very quiet life. Most people in countries like Saudi Arabia, Pakistan and Iran are Moslems. Their god is called Allah. Moslem women had to stay at home. If they left the house they had to put veils over their faces. Some Moslem women lead this sort of life today.

Moslem women at the City Gate in Fez, Morocco

Sharing the work

The farmer and his son go off with the tractor to work in the fields

Some work has always been done by the whole family. In many farming families, everyone helps on the farm. The farmer works in the fields. His wife and children help feed the animals, hens and ducks. At harvest time, men, women and children all work hard to bring in the harvest and neighbours help each other.

The Masai tribe keep herds of cattle in parts of Tanzania and Kenya. They share out the work. The boys and men herd and water the cattle. The women and girls always do the milking.

Feeding lambs from a bottle

Women at work

Does your mother go out to work?

Today many women all over the world go out to work. They do many jobs that only men used to do. In countries like Russia and Britain, women work in factories. They work with the men. In these countries, many women also work in shops and offices.

A carpet-making factory in Ashkhabad, Russia

Tea comes from the leaves of tea bushes. All the tea picking in China, India and Sri Lanka is done by women. The men hoe the ground between the tea bushes to kill the weeds.

Picking tea in Sri Lanka

In Israel, many families live together on village farms. This sort of farm is call a **kibbutz**.
The women work with the men in the orchards. They pick oranges and other fruits. The women also have to join the army.

Harvesting pomegranates in Israel

Helping each other

Not many people can make or grow all the things they need. They need others to help them.

There are tribes of Indians who live in the hot forests by the River Amazon. They manage without help from others.

It is so hot that they do not need much clothing. They build small homes with roofs of palm leaves and no walls. They hunt animals for food and catch fish in the rivers. They gather fruit in the forests. The way they live has not changed for hundreds of years. They do not feel they need to change.

Preparing nets for fishing on a river in the Amazonian jungle

Could you live without help from other people? Most of us could not.

We could not build our own homes without help. We need different workmen to help us. We need bricklayers and carpenters. Think of a typical day in your life. Make a list of all the working people you meet. What would you do without them?

Building houses at Sutton, England

Working round the world

We cannot do everything for ourselves. We need other people to help us. Workers round the world do different jobs. Some produce our food.

Cowboys raise herds of cattle for beef.

Farmers grow wheat for flour to make bread.

Many people grow rice.

Fishermen catch fish for us.

A cattle station at Kimberley, Western Australia

Workers in an electrical factory at Wanganni, on the North Island of New Zealand

Other workers make things. Sometimes they just use their hands. Other things are made with machines.

Workers in factories make our radios and television sets. Our cars are made by workers in other factories.

Some workers entertain us. They dance and sing and make music to make us happy. Actors act plays for us. Authors write the books we read.

Dancers performing at Salakh-Aul in the Krasnodar Territory of Russia

Do you see the postman and milkman every day?

What work does your father do?

What other workers do you see every day?

Make a frieze for your classroom or bedroom wall.
Stick on it pictures of people doing different jobs.

A parcel arriving at a British home

Workers who produce our food

The cattle's thick skin stops them from being burned when the branding mark is made

Farmers

Farmers around the world produce our food. Some keep big herds of cattle. These are killed for beef.

Cowboys

The cowboys of North America work on big farms called ranches. The ranches are on the large grasslands, called **prairies**. Their cattle spend their lives outdoors. They roam wherever they like. The cowboys are good horsemen. They ride many miles each day looking after their cattle. They often eat out in the open. They light a fire and cook a meal of beans, bacon and coffee. At night they sleep in a bunk house. Sometimes they have to stay out at night. Then they just roll up in a blanket and sleep on the ground.

The cowboy puts a branding mark on his animals with a hot iron. This is to stop his cattle getting mixed up with cattle from other ranches. He catches the animals with his **lasso**. This is a rope with a loop at the end.

English dairy farmers

Life on an English dairy farm is not like life on an American ranch. A dairy farm is one where cows are kept for their milk. We all need milk to drink. We also need it to make butter and cheese.

In summer, an English farmer keeps his cows in small fields. There they eat grass. In the winter it is cold. Then the farmer keeps them in cowsheds. He has to give his cows hay, turnips and cowcake to eat.

Each morning and evening he takes his cows into the milking parlour. There he milks them with a machine.

Do you know what happens to your milk before it arrives on your table? Find out as much as you can.

Milking cows by machine. It can be done by hand

Cows stay out day and night in summer

Coal-miners in Wales

Miners usually work for about eight hours at a time. This is called a **shift**.

The miner changes into a boiler suit when he arrives at the mine. He wears a helmet to protect his head. Pads protect his knees. His boots have steel toe-caps.

He is not allowed to take matches or cigarettes with him down the mine.

With the other miners on his shift he goes into a sort of lift called a cage. This is lowered by machinery into the mine. He leaves the cage and goes into one of the tunnels. These are lit by electricity.

The roofs of the tunnels are propped up with steel girders. Giant boring machines are used to dig these tunnels.

Miners at a colliery in Gwent, South Wales. The machine behind them is the winding gear

An underground train at a coal mine in Barnsley, Yorkshire

The men are then taken by trains to the coal face. This is where the coal lies in the rocks.

The miners cut the coal with machines called **power loaders**. The coal is then loaded on to a conveyor belt. This belt moves the coal along steadily to the shaft. It is taken up the shaft and above ground.

A lot of mining today is done by machine. But miners still have to work very hard. Their job is a dangerous one.

At the end of his shift the miner goes to the pithead. He has a bath and changes into clean clothes.

This coal-cutting shearer cuts into the coal

Rubber

Do you bounce rubber balls in the playground? How many things made of rubber do you use every day? Draw some pictures of them.

Do you know what rubber is? Do you know where it comes from?

Natural rubber comes from rubber trees. When the bark of a rubber tree is cut, a sticky juice comes out. This juice is called **latex**. Latex can be made into rubber in special factories.

The lands on which rubber trees are planted are called **rubber plantations**. Rubber trees grow best in hot, wet countries.

There are many rubber plantations in Malaysia, Indonesia, Thailand and Sri Lanka.

The latex collects in a cup below the cut

Think what a hard and bumpy ride you'd have if tyres were not made of rubber!

Rubber trees have thick leaves which keep out some of the sun

Rubber tappers

Many Indians work on plantations in Malaysia. They can earn more money there than in India. It is very hot. They wear cool cotton clothes.

The men who collect the rubber are called tappers. A tapper can tap about four hundred trees each day. He starts work early in the morning, because when the hot sun shines the latex stops flowing.

First, the tapper makes a sloping cut on the tree trunk. He does this with a sharp tool. Then he clips a cup at the end of the cut. The latex trickles slowly into the cup.

By about ten o'clock, the sun stops the latex from flowing. The tappers collect the cups of latex. Then the latex is taken by lorry to the factory. There the latex is turned into rubber. The bales of rubber are sent by ship to other countries.

Making things by machine

Materials like iron and rubber, from which things are made, are called **raw materials**.

In the past, people made things by hand. Now many things are made from raw materials using machines in factories. This is called **manufacturing**. Workers can make things like cars much more quickly by machine.

Latex is made into sheets for packing easily

Making cars

Working on the last stages of an engine for a new car

Have you ever thought how cars are made?
The parts of the cars, like the engines and tyres, are made by people in different factories. Then workers in other factories use these parts to build the cars.

Many cars are manufactured in Britain and Japan.

But before the parts of the cars can be made, the raw materials are needed. Workers in other places have to produce the raw materials. Workers on rubber plantations in countries like Malaysia supply the rubber for tyres.

Miners in countries like Australia and Sweden dig iron ore out of the ground. Steel is then made in factories from the iron ore. Steel is needed for the car bodies and other parts.

Iron ore mining at Iron Knob, South Australia

Turning molten iron ore into steel at a British steel factory

Electricity is needed in factories. It is needed to work the machines. Coal is used in some power stations to make electricity. Miners in countries such as Britain and Australia mine the coal in coal-mines.

You can see that the car industry gives work to thousands of people around the world. Let us look at a few of them at work.

Building the cars

The way people work in car factories is much the same everywhere.

The workers work in shifts. They arrive at the factory. They change into their working clothes. They then go to the **assembly lines**. This is where all the parts of the car are assembled, or put together. All the parts of the car have been made already in other factories. On the assembly line, the frame of the car moves slowly along on a conveyor. The workers stand at different places along the line. They have supplies of all the parts. They attach these to the frame in the right places. The frame reaches the end of the line. Then the car is finished.

Cars on an assembly line at the Ford factory near Liverpool, England

What makes are these cars? Which countries are they from?

Does your family own a car?

If so, what make is it?

Where was it made? Look in newspapers and magazines.

Collect pictures of cars. Stick them in a scrapbook.

Use different pages for cars from different countries.

Japanese car workers

Workers in Japan work very hard indeed. They are loyal to their company. The company looks after them by helping to find them somewhere to live as well as paying their wages.

Cars are made cheaply in Japan because the factories are very efficient.

Russian car workers

All car factories in the USSR are owned by the government. The government is the group of people who rule the country. They also make its laws.

Russian women work in car factories with the men. Some of them live in new blocks of flats in Moscow. This is the capital city of the USSR.

It is cold and snowy in winter. The workers wear thick woollen clothes. They usually travel to work by underground railway or by bus.

The Moskvich 412, a Russian car

They work for only half a day on Saturday. They do not work at all on Sunday.

Russian farm machinery is made at this factory at Rostov-on-Don

British car workers

Some British car workers travel to work on free buses sent by the firm they work for. Other workers travel in their own cars or walk to work. The car workers can earn a lot of money but they have to work hard for it.

The factory owners make sure their workers are healthy. Their factories are kept clean. There is a canteen where the workers can eat.

Some firms give their workers a **pension**. This means that they pay them when they are ill or too old to work anymore. Most car firms have sports and social clubs for workers to relax in or play games after work.

New Ford cars being loaded on to a car transporter

New factories

In the past, only a few countries manufactured their goods. Many sent their raw materials to other countries to be manufactured. India sent raw materials to Britain. Today, many countries have their own factories. They can make their own goods from their own materials.

The Indians grow lots of cotton plants. Now they have built factories. So they can make their own cotton goods.

India makes a lot of cotton cloth.

An open cotton boll

Printing cotton cloth at Rajesthan in India

Factories in Nigeria

In Nigeria, some people still make goods like they did long ago. They make lovely pots, carvings and leather goods by hand. But now the Nigerians are building factories. Here they use their own raw materials. They use cotton, rubber and leather.

Kano is a city in Nigeria. The centre of Kano is still like it was long ago. There are many mud brick houses. The people still make goods by hand. They sell the goods at open-air stalls and markets as they have done for hundreds of years.

These Nigerian women are selling milk

This is a factory making metal cans in Lagos, the capital of Nigeria

But outside Kano, new factories are being built. Some of the factories make shoes.

Richer countries can help poorer countries. They can help them build factories. They can show them how to make things from raw materials. They can help them sell the goods they have made.

We all need help from each other.

Workers who produce our food

This modern trawler is the Northella, and comes from Hull, on the east coast of Britain

Deep sea fishermen

Fishermen from Britain, Norway and Iceland fish in the deep seas around Iceland. They catch cod and herring. Their boats are called **trawlers**. These may be more than thirty metres long. A lot of the space on a trawler is taken up by large fish holds. Here the fish are stored.

You would not enjoy a trip on a trawler very much. You would find the seas around Iceland very cold and rough. A fisherman's life there is very dangerous and difficult.

To keep warm, fishermen wear woollen jerseys. They also wear oilskins to keep out the rain.

A net full of fish. The top is tied with a special knot called a cod-end tie

Trawlers are often at sea for two or three weeks at a time. The crew live on board. They sleep in bunks. The crew is made up of a captain, called 'skipper', the mate, the radio operator, and a cook. There are also three or four deckhands. They look after the nets and fish.

The captain uses special instruments such as a radio and radar. These help him steer the boat safely.

He listens to shipping forecasts on his radio which warn him of gales.

Trawler fishermen catch their fish in large nets called **trawl** nets. These are dragged along the bottom of the seabed.

Look at the picture of the trawler. Use things like corks and egg boxes, scraps of paper and material to make a model of a trawler.

Sorting and cleaning the fish on deck after the catch

Inshore fishermen

In countries that have a sea coast, you will always find fishermen. Britain, Japan and India have sea coasts. There fishermen fish around the coast in small boats.

Their boats are usually small rowing boats. Sometimes they have sails or a motor. In Britain, fishermen in Cornish fishing villages fish for mackerel. They fish in the shallow waters by the coast. They also catch crabs and lobsters in baskets called **pots**.

Fishermen in Japan and India catch prawns. They use a net like a small trawl net with a bar at the bottom.

The sea is dangerous. They never go far from land. They only stay at sea for a few hours at a time.

Fishing boats in the harbour at Newlyn, Cornwall

Other fishermen

Other men fish in rivers, such as the Niger in Nigeria, and in lakes like Lake Chad in Africa.

Nigerian fishermen sometimes use nets fixed to bamboo poles to scoop fish out of the water.

Fishermen in Tanzania use dug-out canoes. Men in the canoe take a long net a little way out to sea. Men on the beach hold the other end. When the fish are in the net they pull the net onto the beach.

On Lake Chad, the fishermen use canoes made from bundles of reeds.

Rod and net fishing on a lake

Hauling in nets on the Caspian Sea, Russia

Sorting nets on the river Niger in Nigeria

The farmer has to fly over his wheat crop to see if it is ripe enough to harvest

Canadian wheat growers

Farmers in Canada grow wheat in large wheat fields. They stretch as far as the eye can see.

It is very cold and snowy in winter. In spring the snow melts. The farm workers use farm machines and tractors to plough the land. They get the soil ready for the seeds.

When the wheat is ripe, the farmers harvest the crop. They use huge machines called **combine harvesters**. The fields are large and do not have any hedges. So more than one harvester is used.

The wide hats protect the workers' heads from the hot sun

Rice farmers in Bangladesh

Most people in Bangladesh are farmers. They only have small farms with small fields called **paddy-fields**. The farmers grow rice in them.

The weather in Bangladesh is hot. It rains heavily in summer. This is good weather for growing rice.

The children and their mothers sow rice in seed beds. During the wet season, the paddy-fields are covered in water. The farmers use water buffalo to pull their ploughs. The rice seeds grow into small plants. Then the children and parents plant the rice seedlings. They plant them in the mud under the water. They wear wide-brimmed hats to protect their heads from the sun.

Planting rice in the wet mud

The hot sun and rich mud help the rice plants to grow quickly. The crop ripens. Then the family cuts the rice with sickles. Farmers in Bangladesh have only their own families to help them. They are too poor to pay wages. They do not earn much money.

The workers work in the fields from early morning until late at night. They do not eat much during the day. They have their big meal in the evening. They eat boiled rice with vegetables or fish. These are cooked in a hot spicy sauce. This is called a curry.

Pretend you live in a village in Bangladesh.

Write a short story about how you help your parents grow rice. Paint a picture to go with your story.

These workers in India are separating the rice grains from the ripe plant

Help for poor farmers

Farm machinery like this tractor can work more quickly than animals

There are many poor farmers in the world. Some live in parts of Africa and India. They keep some animals and grow some crops. They work very hard. But the way they farm is very old-fashioned. The farmers produce hardly enough food to keep their families alive.

They can be helped by other countries in many ways. They can be taught more modern ways of farming.

Some farmers still use oxen to pull their ploughs. They can be given tractors. Then more land can be ploughed and more crops planted.

They can be given fertilisers to make the soil produce better crops. Better seeds and better breeds of animals will help the farmers produce more food to feed their people.

Oxen are cheaper than tractors, but slower

Acknowledgements

The author and publishers wish to acknowledge the following photograph sources:

Agent General for South Australia p.17 (T)
Peter Baker Photography p.26
Baptist Missionary Society p.29 (B)
Barnaby's Picture Library p.28
British Leyland p.16 (B), p.19 (T/R)
British Steel Corporation p.17 (B)
Church Missionary Society p.23 (B)
Compix p.6 (C)
John M. Davis & Associates/Charles Barker p.24 (T/B)
Fiat Motor Company p.19 (T/L)
Fords of Dagenham p.18
Free Chinese Centre p.27 (T)
Government of Western Australia p.8 (T)
Robert Harding Picture Library p.22 (B)
Alan Hutchison Library p.7 (T), p.27 (B)
Japanese Information Centre p.19 (B/R)
Jewish Program & Material Project p.6 (B)
Keystone Press Agency p.7 (B)
The Malaysian Rubber Producers' Research Association p.14 (T), p.15 (plus inset), p.16 (T)
National Coal Board p.12 (B,T&B)
New Zealand Government p.8 (B)
Novosti Press Agency p.9 (T)
Valerie Randall p.4
The Save the Children Fund p.31 (B)
Society for Cultural Relations with the USSR p.6 (T), p.20 (B), p.20 (T), p.27 (C)
Thailand Information Service p.29 (T)
UNICEF p.30
Volkswagen Motors Ltd p.19 (B/L)

The publishers have made every effort to trace the copyright holders, but if they have inadvertently overlooked any, they will be pleased to make the necessary arrangements at the first opportunity.

Illustrations by Brian Watson

© 1981 The Save the Children Fund
and Macmillan Education

All rights reserved

First published 1981

Published by
Macmillan Education Ltd
London and Basingstoke
Associated companies and representatives
throughout the world

Printed in Hong Kong

ISBN 0 333 30677 5